God's Goodness in YOU and ME

By Kelly Kainer Billington

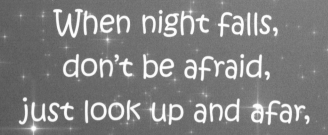

When night falls,
don't be afraid,
just look up and afar,

You will see a
majestic sight from
twinkling star to star.

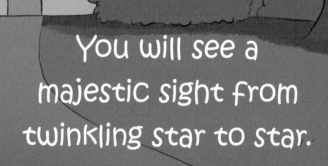

4

You will notice that the night is not totally dark.

God created the Moon to give the night a gentle spark. 5

Rest assured!
When you feel **anger, hate, and fear,**
this could never be Our Lord,
but only his enemy, Satan,
that must be clear!

TO US,
HE is
EVERYTHING!

For
without Him,
we are
NOTHING!

GOD WAS, IS, AND ALWAYS WILL BE!

We see His Goodness throughout the world!

But, especially we see it in YOU and ME!

**I LOVINGLY DEDICATE
THIS BOOK TO**

**MY MOTHER,
MY SON,
MY GRANDSON,
AND MY GOD!**

My beautiful Mother, who so lovingly taught me right from wrong, has been my inspiration in so many ways. The sacrifices she made so her children could have a Christian education were priceless. And she managed to pass on to me the importance of God and family in my life. I know she is smiling in heaven, because she always did!

My Son, who holds one of the most special places in my heart, has always had such a wonderful sense of right and wrong. His heart is as pure as gold, and he has grown to be such a great husband and lovingly devoted father. I am so proud of him and simply could not want for a more awesome son!

My Grandson means the world to me! He has a heart that is as pure as gold and a winning spirit that is undefeatable! There is no doubt that I am a proud Nana indeed! And I could not begin to imagine having a grandson more wonderful than him!

All glory truly goes to God! He has been so good to me!
He is my most beloved inspiration indeed!
And, I am so grateful to Him for blessing me with
My Beautiful Mother,
My Awesome Son,
and My Wonderful Grandson!

ABOUT THE AUTHOR

Kelly Renee Kainer Billington was born in 1961 and raised in Southeast Texas. She is a lovingly devoted wife, mother, and grandmother (Nana), and she advocates that her family and God are most important to her.

She earned her Bachelor of Science degree in Business Administration-Management w/ Teacher Certification. After 12 years in public schools teaching computer and business classes, she felt a calling to enter the real estate world. She became a broker, investor, and renovator and manages the family businesses.

She has written a book named <u>JOY Comes in the Morning</u>, which is a story about a personal journey with her Mother, Alzheimer's, and God. After 12 years of caring for her Mother, she wrote a book in hopes of helping someone experiencing this horrible disease and most importantly to honor God and her Mother, who is her hero.

Kelly advocates that God works in mysterious ways, because <u>God's Goodness in You and Me</u> began when she attended a Disciples in Mission class at her church. As a class assignment, Kelly chose to create a poem about the Goodness of God. She said that she very quickly and simply wrote it in about 30 minutes. When she presented it to the class, the facial expressions and reactions of the people astounded her! They were elated about the poem and went on and on about how wonderful it was! The man sitting next to her said he would love to have a copy of it, so he could frame it. She was totally amazed at the reaction of these good people! A few years later, she had an inspiration to take it from a two-page document and make it into a 15-page children's book.

And that is how <u>God's Goodness in You and Me</u>, and an author, if you will, was born. As Kelly steps into her future as an author, she hopes to help and inspire people of all ages with her publications!

Kelly Kainer Billington

Notes

Notes

Notes

Notes

WestBow Press books may be ordered through booksellers or by contacting:

WestBow Press
A Division of Thomas Nelson & Zondervan
1663 Liberty Drive
Bloomington, IN 47403
www.westbowpress.com
1 (866) 928-1240

ISBN: 978-1-9736-3532-1 (sc)
ISBN: 978-1-9736-3533-8 (e)

Library of Congress Control Number: 2018908909

Print information available on the last page.

WestBow Press rev. date: 01/21/2019

WestBow
PRESS®
A DIVISION OF THOMAS NELSON
& ZONDERVAN

Printed in the United States
By Bookmasters